Through calm or conflict,
Faith or fear,
Success or stillness,

The flag of our nation
continues to wave...

-SW

Published by A Matter of Rhyme, Killeen, TX
Library of Congress Control Number: 2021915070
www.amatterofrhyme.com
For event and educational information contact
sheri@amatterofrhyme.com

Printed in the United States of America
First Printing, 2021
ISBN # 978-1-7330943-7-5

To Kennedy,

Hooray for the USA!

Our Pledge Our Promise

The Pledge of Allegiance Explained

Sheri Wall

by Sheri Wall   art by Gary Manly

Most children have heard it

And repeated it too.

But why do we pledge

To the Red, White, and Blue?

Old Glory, a nickname,
The flag of our states.
United in freedom,
We can all celebrate.

"I pledge allegiance"

I promise to be loyal

Right hand over heart,

Please stand while reciting.

We're ready to start.

"To the flag"

To the symbol of the United States

Our own stars and stripes,

Its beauty waves grandly

In dawn's early light.

"Of the United States of America"

A country of 50 states

All fifty we count,
From East Coast to West Coast,
Up north and down south.

N
W
E
S

“And to the Republic”

To our democratic country

We vote for our dreams.

A government where people

Hold power supreme.

VOTE
VOTE
VOTE

"For which it stands"

Which it represents

Flag and country connect.
We make a promise
To show due respect.

SOCIAL STUDIES
MATH

“One Nation under God”

A country of religious freedom

We should all rise above

And care for our neighbors,

Together with love.

DONATE
FOOD

“Indivisible”

Joined together always

We won’t break or bend.

Our country is worthy,

With pride we defend.

“With liberty and justice”

With freedom and fair treatment

Our freedoms are fair.

Opportunities are many,

The truth we do share.

“For all”

For every person who lives here

We must understand,

Each one is included

Throughout our great land.

It only takes seconds

To say every day.

So very important,

The American way.

I PLEDGE ALLEGIANCE TO THE FLAG OF THE UNITED STATES OF AMERICA AND TO THE REPUBLIC FOR WHICH IT STANDS, ONE NATION UNDER GOD, INDIVISIBLE, WITH LIBERTY AND JUSTICE FOR ALL.

The next time you hear
Our pledge said aloud,
Join in with a big voice,
Unite and be proud!

Fun Facts

1777 - Congress, the lawmaking branch of the United States government, voted to use The Stars and Stripes as the flag of America on June 14th. The original version had one star and one stripe for each of the thirteen original colonies.

1818 - It was decided that instead of adding a star and a stripe for each new state, the stripes would return to thirteen in honor of the original colonies, and only the stars would increase.

1831 - The nickname "Old Glory" was first used by sea captain William Driver for his personal flag.

1885 - A small-town Wisconsin teacher named Bernard Cigrand originated the idea of an annual flag day to be celebrated every June 14th.

1892 - Minister Francis Bellamy wrote the original Pledge of Allegiance.

1923 - The words "the Flag of the United States of America" were added by Congress.

1945 - The official name of The Pledge of Allegiance was adopted.

1954 - The words of the Pledge of Allegiance were changed again to add "under God," which is the version we still use today.

1954 - On March 1st, President Dwight Eisenhower issued a proclamation as to the proper times to fly the flag at half-staff, which shows the country is in mourning or sad about a loss.

1958 - The current flag containing 50 stars and 13 stripes and designed by high school student Robert G. Heft of Lancaster, Ohio.

1969 - On July 20th, Astronaut Neil Armstrong placed an American flag on the moon as part of the first manned landing on the moon, Apollo 11.

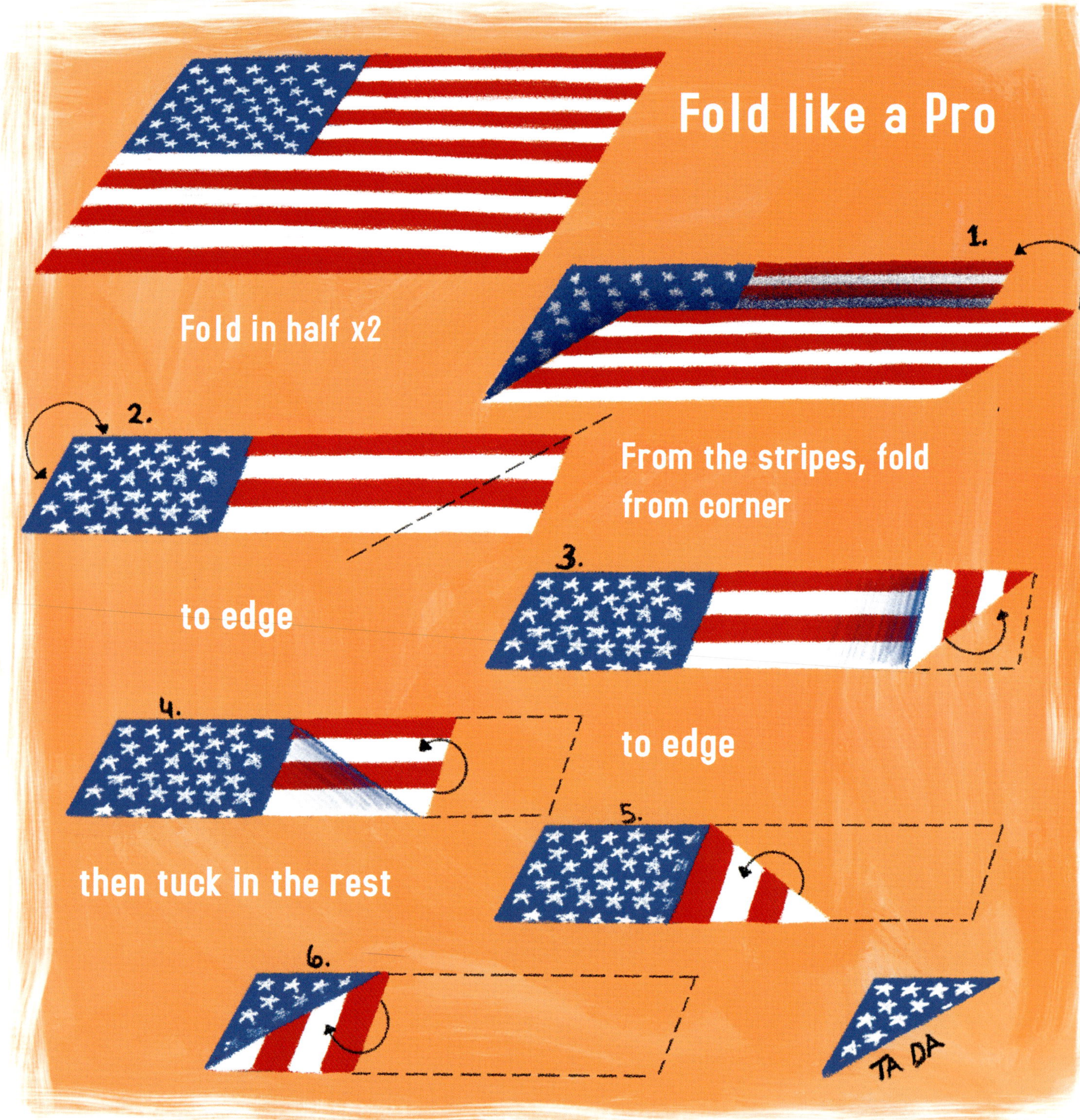
Fold like a Pro
1.
Fold in half x2
2.
From the stripes, fold
from corner
3.
to edge
4.
to edge
5.
then tuck in the rest
6.
TA DA

Red means hardiness and
valor. Bold and brave,
the red stripes wave.
White means purity
and innocence.
Free and clear, truths
we hold dear.
Blue means vigilance,
perseverance, and justice.
Side by side, the stars will ride.

Sheri Wall is a lover of rhyme who has lived in Texas for a really long time. She would read to her sons and kids that she knew, and they all enjoyed rhyming picture books too. Then A Matter of Rhyme began as a dream to help others learn with zippy rhyme schemes. Sheri likes to stay active and be on the go, either biking, shopping, or seeing a show. To find more lively books by this witty mom, visit her website amatterofrhyme.com.

Gary Manly is a freelance illustrator, and graphic designer who lives in Belton, Texas with his beautiful wife and two crazy kids. In his free time Gary loves to paint, play the ukuele, and travel with his family.

Follow Gary on
Facebook@garymanlyart
Instagram@garymanly